Introduction

Tourism is the world's biggest industry.

The World Tourism Organisation estimates that it employs up to 10% of the world's workforce, and accounts for 10% of global gross domestic product.

Its scale makes the industry difficult to comprehend. This is compounded by its bewildering variety. And by the sector's phenomenal growth rate – among both international and domestic tourists.

This document doesn't attempt to engage with the industry as a whole. Instead, *Changing Nature Tourism* concentrates on:

— nature tourism – the enduring appeal to tourists of the world's great nature sites

in

— developing countries – visited by around 3 million UK travellers every year

and

— actions that organisations – private, public and not-for-profit – can take to influence nature tourism.

Multiple challenges, triple bottom line

As tourism overtakes oil to claim the crown of biggest industry on earth, it is *inevitable* that its behaviour and its sustainability will be closely scrutinised. And as other businesses have discovered, glossy brochures (even of attractive holiday destinations) aren't enough.

Nature tourism has especially important responsibilities. It is the only industry allowed to develop in many of the world's great natural sites. It will survive only by protecting the natural resource base on which it depends. And it needs the support of the people who live in its destinations if it is to continue to thrive.

Imaginative tourism businesses, like those in other industries, look to the future – and act in the present. They are increasingly facing up to the challenge of the 'triple bottom line'. This accepts that economic, environmental *and* social factors must all be attended to *simultaneously*.

As John Elkington, a leading writer on sustainability issues and business, puts it: "To refuse the challenge implied by the triple bottom line is to risk extinction. Nor are these simply issues for major transitional corporations: they will increasingly be forced to pass the pressure on down their supply chains, to smaller suppliers and contractors."

This is not an issue faced just by the private sector. Many national parks emerged from purely environmental concerns – and still have the scars to prove it. Keoladeo National Park in India – a man-made wetland created to provide a royal duck shoot – provides a good instance. Declared a protected area in 1982, villagers were deprived of rights to graze cattle and collect thatching grass. The gates in the perimeter wall were shut – denying one village its main access to market. In the resulting unrest, seven villagers died. 16 years later, local people are still paying – in lost access to resources – to conserve the park.

Conservationists have now, by and large, abandoned such exclusion policies – not least because they proved environmentally counter-productive. In Zimbabwe, for instance, the Mahenye people concluded that if all the elephants could be destroyed, the authorities would lose interest in the area – and they would get their land back. 'Shadrak' became a local folk hero – by heading a team of poachers, and by killing 20 to 30 large bull elephants every year, for 15 years.

Use-it-or-lose-it conservation strategies aim to achieve their goals through increased access – and tourism is a key component. Yet local people *must* benefit if they are to have a stake in a park's future.

The triple bottom line offers other challenges to civil societies. Just as the tourism business has been accused of neglecting its environmental and social 'bottom lines', so NGOs, development agencies and government organisations are all facing calls to bring a sharper economic edge to their work. In tourism, this translates into a need to grasp the business agenda – to understand the industry as it is now *and* to help local entrepreneurs create new tourism businesses.

Sustainability offers one more challenge – communication. Sustainable development is currently poorly understood by the UK public, and organisations need to work hard to explain how the triple bottom line is changing the way we see the world.

DEPARTURES

Changing *the* Nature *of* Tourism

Developing an agenda for action

air Britain

Outbound

Changing Nature Tourism uses new DFID research as the basis of discussion.

The research was carried out by the University of Kent's Durrell Institute of Conservation and Ecology (DICE) and is available on paper from Tourism Concern, or electronically from the DFID website (www.dfid.gov.uk). *Tourism, Conservation and Sustainable Development: Case Studies from Asia and Africa* describes the main conclusions and is available from IIED. See *Signposts* for contact details.

The research compared three very different nature tourism destinations:

Keoladeo National Park in India
> an internationally important wetland situated in the Golden Triangle, best known for its (elusive) Siberian Cranes

Komodo National Park in Indonesia
> a spice island which is both a popular cruise-ship destination and part of an independent travellers' route through Indonesia to Australia. Komodo is most famous for its monitor dragons (*Varanus komodoensis*)

The south-east Lowveld in Zimbabwe
> a safari destination just opening to tourists. It includes the Gonarezhou National Park, three private wildlife conservancies, a charitable trust, a commercial lease farm and a major CAMPFIRE (Communal Areas Management Programme for Indigenous Resources) development

The research explores who visits these destinations (and why); how much they spend (and where that money goes); and looks at the involvement and responses of both the local community and the industry. It asks how the impact of visitors can be managed more effectively, and describes barriers to local involvement in the tourism industry.

The issues raised, and many of the research findings, are not restricted to state-owned land – though national parks and protected areas have a central role in the nature tourism sector. Neither does the term 'nature tourism' imply travel only to pristine wildernesses. Indeed Keoladeo, while beautiful and rich in biodiversity, is man-made – and almost every place a tourist visits has a local community that calls it home.

The research study findings were further enriched by three consultation conferences, with key players from the tourism industry, the media, and government & non-government organisations (NGOs).

The conferences highlighted the difficulties that all parties have in grappling with a rapidly growing industry. Given this fast-changing landscape, *Changing Nature Tourism* concentrates on provoking debate and stimulating new thinking. It closes with a possible agenda for action by each sector.

This agenda is necessarily a preliminary one. Nevertheless, the research and consultation findings suggest that there *are* actions – large and small – which can be taken. A strategic vision is emerging about how nature tourism can help rural communities in developing countries. Communities who, for generations, have helped shape and protect the natural wonders we are so keen to see.

The DFID agenda

DFID brings a clear approach to *Changing Nature Tourism*.

In its 1997 White Paper, the department committed itself to helping reduce world poverty by half by 2015 – and recently DFID has commissioned work to explore the contribution that tourism can make to this goal.

Nature tourism is a dynamic market, experiencing faster-than-average growth in a burgeoning sector. It is well placed to offer a viable source of income for rural communities – income which can have a major impact on extremely poor communities. Nature tourism can also deliver much-needed improvements to rural infrastructure and services – in turn encouraging further development.

The challenge, however, is to ensure the benefits of tourism are sustainable and fairly distributed – and any negative impacts are minimised.

The key issues for nature tourism are to ensure that:

- **local communities play a role in its development and management – and secure a fair share of its benefits**

- **destinations receive long-term investment and commitment from operators – providing economic stability**

- **the industry contributes to conserving the natural resource base on which it depends**

Cutting the cake

Tourism has been seized on as a way that important natural sites can secure revenue to reduce management costs.

Yet DFID's research showed how *little* money many National Parks make from tourism. While it costs about US$300 for a two-night trip from Bali or Lombok to see Komodo's dragons, the park gets just 70 cents of this. Gonarezhou (US$5) and Keoladeo (83 cents) also have relatively cheap daily entrance fees.

Before a park's income and expenditure can be compared, it is necessary to decide exactly what should be counted as *tourism-related* expenditure. DFID's research illustrates this point with measures from opposite ends of the spectrum.

The first includes *only* money spent on facilities and services intended *exclusively* for tourists (administration of ticket sales, provision of picnic areas, etc.).

The second works from the argument that many parks are now run solely for the benefit of foreign, national and local visitors (especially given that other economic uses, such as grazing and fuel collection, have been disallowed). *All* park expenditure is therefore considered to be tourism-related.

By the first measure, of the three parks only Keoladeo raises enough income from entrance fees to generate a surplus. The other parks studied run deficits, with facilities for tourists subsidised at Gonarezhou by 17 cents per visitor and at Keoladeo by 4 cents.

By the second measure, all three parks run a considerable deficit: $1.84 per tourist in Keoladeo; $13.40 per tourist on Komodo; and $15.78 per tourist in Gonarezhou.

With the truth probably somewhere between the two – and parks under increasing pressure to become self-financing – it is clear that prices are likely to rise. When asked, most tourists seemed to understand this: 60% would accept an *eight-fold* increase in the Komodo entrance fee, and 80% a doubling at Gonarezhou.

Both tourists and tour operators want a *much* clearer sense of where their money goes. The evidence suggests that price rises will be more acceptable when there are clear signals that ticket sales directly contribute to the area being visited – either the park itself, rural development projects nearby, or in the case of heavily visited parks, other less-popular parks.

The role of national parks

Tourism is currently mainly controlled in *originating* countries – many *destination* countries need a stronger institutional structure if they are to play a stronger role.

This makes national parks, and similar protected areas, important players. They are already centres of institutional strength and can act as a focus for tourism development, especially in rural areas.

Many protected areas already take tourism very seriously – with at least three-quarters of parks allowing for tourism in their management plans. But tourism will grow in importance as managers face pressure to reduce dependency on national taxation *and* provide local communities with a fairer share of benefits derived from the natural resource.

Through tourism, park managers can:

— increase direct income – by higher admission charges and other fees

— help create an environment in which local tourism businesses can thrive

— offer local people new employment opportunities in the park

Money talks

Different types of tourist have quite different impacts.

Some domestic tourists may spend less money *overall* but, research shows, they often spend more in the local economy. In parks like Keoladeo, where they make up 70% of all visitors, anything which discourages them from travelling would have disproportionate effects on the area's poorest people.

Foreign tourists also act in very different ways. DFID looked at the spending of different groups in Komodo, for instance. While independent travellers (often backpackers on tight budgets) spend nearly $100 locally per visit, package holidaymakers spend only half this. Cruise-ship arrivals, meanwhile, spent on average just *three cents* in the local economy.

An increase in park admission charges could therefore have unwelcome (and unintended) effects if not carefully managed. In many parks, price increases are likely to stop some independent travellers from coming, or to result in shorter visits.

Parks, like all tourism businesses, can make a big difference by adopting a different attitude to the informal economy. At Keoladeo, for instance, small businesses near the gate depend on the *unofficial* sanction of park staff. *Official* support would make a big difference to the stability and development of these traders – and offer opportunities for new ones.

Dismantling market barriers is one way to encourage people to seize new opportunities. Big businesses often refuse to source locally because supplies cannot be guaranteed. Yet a wholesale market, for example, can quickly change this situation.

Businesses need to think about how *they* can develop their supply chain. They have the marketing and logistic skills. Schemes to pass these skills on offer exciting possibilities. After all, many of the world's strongest companies have gained commercial advantage by cultivating strong local links. Tomorrow's tourism businesses need to do the same.

Visitor management

Many parks need assistance in improving visitor management.

For tourist management plans to be realistic, they need clearly articulated and agreed limits to the 'acceptable change' a park can tolerate. Agreed indicators can then be used to measure progress (or otherwise).

Management solutions are also needed for simple, but persistent, problems such as litter. Improved financial controls – perhaps deriving from a more direct link between park income and expenditure – will also be necessary, particularly as income increases.

To help each park make key decisions, good-quality market information is needed. Important issues include:

— how the market segments into different types of visitor

— what each market segment represents in terms of positive (and negative) economic, social and environmental impacts – both on the park and on surrounding communities

— how changes in tourism management will change the market profile

— what effect a change in the market profile will have – especially on the informal economy

Box camera

Tourists travel – and arrive – both in hope, and with great expectations. Armed with cameras, they see wonderful places crying out to be snapped. Yet the locals, who live there, have their own perceptions. In Keoladeo, for instance, the locals believe that the wetland was closed for grazing on the advice of foreigners, 'who did not want to be disturbed taking photos'. And when the park's most famous bird, the Siberian Crane, made a (now) rare appearance, two tourists and a forester came to blows. (The argument was over who should be allowed closest... to take photographs.)

Tour operators see through a different lens again. They see *customers*, who they hope will come back, pass on favourable reports – and not prove too 'difficult'. (There's always one.) They need to be confident of success before embracing change. 'Will a new project provide consistent levels of customer satisfaction?' is a question they ask.

Governments see through a much wider-angled lens, looking at foreign currency flows and strategic development. NGOs, meanwhile, often offer a 'close-up', working in local communities on complex issues that the average visitor is unlikely to be aware of at all.

All these points of view have validity and can make for creative differences. Yet as numbers of nature tourists increase, so does the need to understand their impact and the benefits they offer – and to whom. From all points of view.

One way to facilitate creative understanding is through guiding. It's a good example of a relatively easy, low-cost approach. Guiding provides *local* employment in communities facing urban drift, and gives visitors a richer understanding of the local environment and culture. Importantly, it also gives *communities* a sense of ownership. (It's very different showing a stranger round your home to having a stranger show a stranger round.) Liaison costs may be higher and training sometimes needed, but an enhanced relationship with the local community brings additional benefits – from a better awareness of game movements to a more welcoming atmosphere.

There's plenty of evidence – and the research uncovered more – that nature tourists *enjoy* informative interactions with local people. In Keoladeo, for instance, 62% considered a local guide their *main* source of learning. This compared to 19% learning most from their tour guide – who is unlikely to be local.

By placing added value on local stories, experiences, practices and activities, local guiding also helps to secure cultural diversity. Meanwhile, nature tourists are more likely to leave feeling they have visited somewhere, and not simply passed through.

Establishing a more localised relationship between visitors and the attraction's community is a starting point for other developments. Skills are likely to develop, opportunities to emerge (and be identified as such), and other forms of cross-pollination to occur. One suggestion involves 'Friends of the Park' schemes, where the national park acts as an authoritative and credible institution to help foster relationships and exchanges. In another, parks use their credibility to provide shipping and insurance services for the kind of larger, higher value items – from furniture to sculpture – that many tourists might buy if confident their purchase was secure.

Community involvement

Many communities are enthusiastic about the *potential* of tourism – but face a variety of barriers to participation.

Around Gonarezhou National Park in Zimbabwe, for instance, 95% of people support tourism to the park and 82% want more contact with tourists. However, most currently feel excluded from the benefits. 54% believe the park is 'for outsiders', and 64% think tourism brings money only to those who are already wealthy.

Research also shows that growing numbers of tourists would like more meaningful contact with local communities. Diversifying to meet this demand could provide low-cost economic opportunities for local people, creating a more rounded and sustainable tourism product.

This list of tourism-related enterprises from the Zimbabwean Lowveld (some already operating, others being developed or discussed) gives an idea of the opportunities:

— Manufacture and supply of building materials

— Uniform manufacture

— Food and vegetable production

— Game meat retail and distribution

— Furniture manufacture

— Curio manufacture

— Guiding services

— Transport

— Sale and distribution of fuelwood

— Cultural tourism activities

— Traditional show village

— Community-based wildlife projects

— Accommodation joint ventures

The small business business

Tourism is a big industry based on small business. And while significant major players offer large numbers of popular packages, even in mass destinations the small businesses are the bedrock of visitors' experiences. The importance of small businesses to nature tourism in rural areas of developing countries cannot be overstated. Although fast-growing, this niche market does not generally offer the kind of turnover and visitor flow needed to attract the major operators.

Britain has considerable expertise and institutional capacity in this area, much of which could be developed and translated for developing world contexts on a partnership basis. Various packages of tourism and small business training modules could enter formal and informal education – and their provision could even, of course, become a viable small business in itself.

There are many opportunities: for governments and donor agencies to foster an entrepreneurial climate; for NGOs and others to develop and deliver skills and training packages; and for industry to work in partnerships (and through routes such as mentoring schemes) to strengthen the overall business base. Interestingly, current work in the Philippines suggests that when small tourism businesses start working together – through market associations, chambers of commerce and so on – real momentum can build.

This idea of small businesses needing a multiplier effect is noted in *The Entrepreneurial Society* – a report that has had a great influence on policy towards small business in *this* country: "A healthy flow of good quality new businesses is necessary for a dynamic economy. Such enterprises renew the existing stock, innovate, found entirely new industries and create employment. Entrepreneurs are a key force in this development, spotting market opportunities and bringing together people and resources."

Capital is always important. In the UK, the Prince's Trust has used small amounts of credit (tied to carefully designed support programmes) to offer loans to individuals initially rejected by the major banks. Their success and repayment rates far outpace those same banks. Meanwhile, in Bangladesh, the Grameen Bank (see *Signposts*) reversed conventional banking practice by removing the need for collateral. So far it has loaned $2.5 billion to over 2 million members. Other micro-credit schemes have also demonstrated powerful results in developing countries. The message – that dedicated and energetic entrepreneurs, appropriate support, and micro-credit make sense – is now a major force for change. (The Prince of Wales Business Leaders Forum – see *Signposts* – has a large reserve of case studies and partnership materials.)

Robert Gavron, Marc Cowling, Gerald Holtham & Andrea Westhall (1998) *The Entrepreneurial Society*, Institute for Public Policy Research, London.

Small business

For local communities, tourism can be difficult to break into. With larger projects requiring capital investment on a scale seldom available locally, the barriers to getting involved can seem insuperable.

Small business offers a solution. Lower levels of capital are needed and risks can be more easily managed. In the UK, tourism supports large numbers of small businesses – and considerable resources and expertise are devoted to encouraging them.

There is potential for similar work in developing countries. Input is needed from organisations who *understand* the business agenda – and who can identify, and work with, potential entrepreneurs.

Evidence from business support projects in developed countries suggests that entrepreneurs need:

— basic skills such as financial planning and book-keeping

— marketing skills, to understand both potential demand – and how to meet it

— access to small amounts of capital, through micro-credit or loan-guarantee schemes

— a supportive environment in which to operate, especially the presence of similar businesses to help create local entrepreneurial 'hot spots'

Global information position

Globalisation is a powerful contemporary phenomenon – one with increasing cultural, as well as economic, impacts. Not all these are positive. Research evidence shows a narrowing of people's future horizons, a growing suspicion of most institutions (including many charities), and a resultant lessening of interest in what is happening in the world.

This is disastrous for developmentalists and bad news, too, for large sections of the media who see their job as expanding horizons. Tourism, of course, offers many people their single most *positive* interaction with the wider world. The challenge is to help people bring these cultural links back home. It is one that needs to be taken up not just by campaigning NGOs, developmental educationalists and the media – but by developing countries themselves.

Better information can help address a different – but related – issue: how the tourist behaves while away. Today's consumer must be *encouraged* to be more discriminating. For how else will people get tourist operators competing to meet values other than simply price? Informed consumers will also think more carefully about what demands are reasonable. Saving water and energy by reducing the number of towels used in hotel rooms has become a cliché – but only because notices have made a difference in hotels around the world.

Many nature tourists do not expect, in a poor rural area, the facilities found in rich cities. Some *enjoy* roughing it for a while, and are even prepared to pay more for the privilege. Certain standards will always remain non-negotiable though – especially security and basic hygiene.

With 60% of all tourist choices thought to be based on word-of-mouth, it is important not to raise expectations that cannot be met. Currently, some tourists come to Komodo National Park looking for a cheap place to stay. The accommodation, however, was originally intended for emergency use and cannot cope with the demand. In this case, it might be better to stop overnight stays, and concentrate resources on shorter but more fulfilling visits.

Where nature tourists do want a better service, their demands are usually fairly modest. Better interpretation is often at the top of the list. Research shows people generally do not want expensive visitor centres, but instead prefer simple (and cheap) options such as information labels, and hides for viewing wildlife. In an innovative partnership, Dartmoor Park Authority are working with counterparts in Nepal to show what can be done. They are producing useful and informative leaflets for tourists to several Nepalese attractions – which then generate income for the local people who sell them.

Visitor education is also critical in ensuring tourists' behaviour is sensitive to local cultures. Problems with inappropriate dress are well known. Other issues include problems caused by tourists using out-dated guidebook information refusing to pay current prices, and people haggling traders down to levels that threaten their livelihood.

A range of outlets is available for this kind of information. A current initiative by Voluntary Services Overseas (VSO) shows the potential of in-flight videos and magazines. New media such as the internet also offer enormous possibilities. Better and *locally* produced information offers scope for effective business partnerships.

Consumer action

The development of the tourism industry will continue to be driven by the attitudes of its consumers – more sustainable nature tourism products are therefore dependent on *their* agenda.

Nature tourists, unsurprisingly, book holidays because they want contact with natural environments and the people who live in them.

Most are spending a significant proportion of their income, and this translates into exacting standards and heightened expectations. They are therefore likely to be sensitive to suggestions that their holiday harms the environment or fails to benefit local communities.

And as other industries, such as agriculture and oil, have found, underestimating the power of the modern consumer can be catastrophic.

Honest relations with consumers are essential – quite simply, people react badly when they feel they have not been told the whole story.

Consumers therefore need better information on:

— who benefits from the money they spend

— the environmental impacts of their trip – and efforts to mitigate them

— the importance of their behaviour while abroad

Holiday I

An ounce of action

As Engels said, "an ounce of action is worth a ton of theory", so throughout the process of preparing this document DFID has concentrated on asking stakeholders what they think can be *done* to help develop nature tourism sustainably.

As well as some practical ideas (see the following three sections), there is common ground as to *what* different groups can do over the next few years – to protect their interests (or those of people they represent) and to realise nature tourism's potential (while minimising its costs).

Businesses involved in nature tourism will be:

- protecting their product: by helping ensure a future for irreplaceable natural resources

- developing a 'licence to operate': by building support, at all levels, for tourism in areas where many *other* activities are curtailed

- strengthening their brand: by building on consumer identification with environmental and social goals

The media will be:

- pushing the world's biggest industry higher up the news and investigative agenda

- considering the ethics and responsibilities of specialist travel journalism, particularly in terms of the relationship of travel writers with the industry

- considering how guidebooks should use the enormous influence they exert in nature tourism destinations

Governmental organisations and NGOs, meanwhile, will be:

- developing coherent policy to reflect tourism's challenges

- working with industry to learn about the realities shaping available choices, while helping create an environment in which higher standards can be delivered

- using links with local communities to help develop more informed choices

Action will not be carried out alone – partnership is, of course, important. Industry will work more closely with NGOs – benefiting from their knowledge of what is wanted, what works and what doesn't. Government, meanwhile, will be developing more ambitious public/private partnerships.

The media, too, will benefit from closer contact with other groups. Currently, they lack effective briefing to help them develop new angles on what is a complex and fascinating debate.

Tourism is based on global communications – change in the industry will, no doubt, follow the same routes.

Action points

Informing the consumer makes sense only if there is progress to report. In tourism, as in any industry, there is clearly much work to be done.

— The tourism industry bears the main responsibility for developing nature tourism. It faces pressure from the media, governments, NGOs and the people who live in its destinations.

Perhaps the most serious challenges, however, will come from within – as pioneering companies reap a competitive advantage.

— The media provide a critical conduit for information about tourism. Well placed to shape consumer understanding and expectations, the media also have a responsibility to developing countries – whose complex realities have not always been well reported.

— Finally, while government and non-governmental organisations continue to act as advocates for fairer tourism, they can also play an important role by helping to deliver results. Civil society is just beginning to get to grips with the scale and importance of the tourism industry – further engagement offers real opportunities for change.

The Interactive Age

Give clients access to local culture. The demand is there. Possibilities include craft markets, food, entertainment, guided tours, village walks, information and other 'lifestyle' products.

Target younger clients. Alert to the issues, young people want new products – with a 'fair tourism' angle – aimed at them. They grow up, become wealthier – and are the future of the business.

Work with national parks as 'credible' institutions. Joint partnerships could work on promotion and publicity; shipping large and high-value craft, furniture, sculpture, etc.; developing websites and Friends of the Park schemes.

Loyalty

Explore longer-term investments. Communities and nature sites are not 'consumables'. Consistency, reliability and loyalty are business and product strengths – which can rub off on clients.

Help clients maintain links with destinations. Ideas include 'adopt a project' (or two), 'adopt a habitat', regular newsletters, sponsorships, promoting school exchanges or 'twinning' schemes.

Develop schemes where a small sum of money is added to the price of a holiday, tour etc. Channel income directly to the project – and then tell clients why you're doing it and how it's going.

Run a 'spare binocular' scheme. Encourage clients to bring a spare for game wardens and local guides. And if clients forget, make arrangements for UK collection. Extend scheme to other items.

Purchasing Power

Deliberately choose locally sourced goods and services if possible. Where there are barriers (e.g. no local wholesale market) use contacts and influence to help remove them.

Encourage local hotels and hotel chains to use their sales outlets to market locally produced goods.

Pass on the pressure down the supply line: get hotels, suppliers, rental firms and others to act, too. Push to get tourism involved in the UK Ethical Trade Initiative.

Act as a conduit for information. Use company materials (e.g. leaflets) to mention local community business projects – or use influence to help place them in other outlets such as airports and hotels.

Think Global, Act Local

Promote local guiding and local knowledge (e.g. current locations of wildlife, characters of individual animals) to create a more authentic product.

Consider 'in kind' benefits. From sharing basic marketing ideas, business expertise, photocopying and photography, to offering access to supplies and services in the UK – cash is not the only scarce resource.

Invest in the future. Micro-credit is about very small amounts of capital making a large difference. Default rates are extremely low. Consider making credit available yourself – or offering a guarantee.

Share better practice. Co-operate to identify, refine and share better practice. Competing won't always work.

Follow the rules. Official guiding systems offer minimum standards – but are weakened when businesses go the unofficial route. Local people can't be expected to be happy if operators allow their tourists to illegally cut wood.

The Training Gain

Train the businesses of tomorrow. Transfer skills from UK businesses to new developing country enterprises, run mentoring schemes, take on job placements. Investing in local partnerships can bring rich rewards.

Invest in staff training. Sustainability and triple-bottom-line issues demand a more informed staff – who in turn can communicate the new agenda to clients, who like to learn. Exert such efforts at all levels of the company.

Look at formal education, e.g. the tourism National Vocational Qualification (NVQ) structure, to develop the new skills and knowledge needed by the next generation in the business.

Inform Action

Recognise the importance of information. From brochures to information offered by tour guides, points of contact offer key chances to create more considerate and responsive clients.

Review existing promotional materials. Show local people and culture – not just 'nature'.

Provide 'labels' to inform clients. Flagging social and environmental impacts sends positive and active signals about the company, raises general awareness – and informs the clientele.

Support certification. Back up ethical claims and profit from growing demand for ethical products. Get certified. Use labels that give consumers the information they need.

Promote independent award schemes. They're a focus for high standards – the publicity is good for business, too.

Examine all available contacts with clients. From original advertising and brochures to ticket wallets and tour information. Use them to make change happen.

Provide information resources locally. Or use 'in-house' skills and resources to help local projects to develop more professional information resources of their own.

Work Together

Pool resources and expertise. Consider working together a *group* of operators on a larger project.

Sign-up to a Code of Ethics. Help develop it, and apply peer pressure to make it a success.

The Media Agenda

Key Messages

Mainstream tourism. The biggest industry in the world isn't just about where's best to eat or get a tan. There are plenty of fresh news, business and consumer stories waiting there.

Be more critical. The realities of travel affect readers too. Most of the media have yet to even leave the airport ('airport strike chaos') when reporting the downside of tourism.

Explore ambiguities. Travel is never unadulterated pleasure. *All* visitors sometimes feel uncomfortable in poor countries. More thoughtful work will help readers deal with the real world.

Reinvigorate the issues. Good journalists should never see issues as simply 'worthy', 'preachy' or boring. It should help to find out what's important and what's cant – and to write about both.

Create new narratives. There is no single overarching narrative conveying the complexity of nature tourism. It's open territory, which is exciting.

Push tourism up the lifestyle agenda. It worked with food and restaurants. Average spending on travel and tourism is already high – and rising.

New Angles

Encourage better briefing. Remind industry and organisation contacts of the mutual value of detailed media briefs.

Find new angles. The media can widen interest using new pegs: enormous industries merit investigative journalism – what is value-for-money (and for whom)?

Develop more substantial (even investigative) pieces. There are some very big stories waiting to happen – these will raise the profile of the sector (and the media involved).

Use media diversification. Tourism content is well suited to new TV channels, radio, magazines and other new outlets. It offers good pictures, interesting sounds, real people and cultural depth.

Try the public information route. Tourism training and information would be very useful. Radio is a good medium in the developing world (what about a World Service soap for global impact)?

Open out travel and tourism conceptually. The 'industry of our age' talks to where we are going, and why – more open territory awaiting exploration.

Use tourism to bring other issues to life. Poverty. Development. The environment. What they are – and what they mean.

Ethics

Declare interests (e.g. 'freebies'). The Nolan Committee leads the way: the media should match Parliamentary standards of probity and integrity. Readers have a right to know what's advertorial, what hospitality was offered, and so on. Good practice exists – it should be universal. A Code of Practice might help.

Educate picture editors. An important issue, often overlooked. Photography has *direct* ethical responsibilities (e.g. a Muslim woman may be shunned by her village if it's known she appeared in a press photo) and *indirect* ones (e.g. representing people or culture, not just nature or glamour).

Avoid reinforcing prejudice. Old clichés (e.g. 'trouble in paradise') are poor work, and do no favours to writer *or* reader.

Network with southern journalists. If you use their local knowledge, language skills and contacts, return the favour to help them place stories in northern outlets. The *quid pro quo* is more easily forgotten at a distance; and is more important to remember, too.

Guidebooks

Trust readers more. Guidebooks are sometimes nicknamed 'The Bible'. The Reformation is overdue. Remove some of the mystique about how guidebooks are put together. Readers will then have more realistic expectations – and be open to new options which the guide doesn't cover.

Ensure guidebook accuracy. Given that travellers frequently use outdated information to refuse to pay today's prices, guidebooks are indirectly pushing *costs* onto already very poor people. If accuracy is impossible, say so – often.

Use influence. Readers don't like lectures – but they do like experts. Look at how 'The Bible' can be used to convey useful *general* and *specific* messages (e.g. top tips, the 10 Commandments, expert dos and don'ts).

Consider new partnerships. The Internet and other media offer opportunities to work together: the Rough Planet or Lonely Guide could provide a powerful voice for a new generation of travellers – and their interests.

Use best practice. Modern readers *do* want to know about their impact, and how to engage more successfully with countries they visit. Experts – i.e. seasoned travel writers – tend to forget how much they know, and others don't. Research readers' changing needs.

Governments

Identify strategic priorities. DFID will work with all its partners to help them identify strategic priorities which can shape better nature tourism.

Plug the global policy gap. Tourism policy needs an authoritative international voice.

Create legal or regulatory frameworks. Because tourism cuts across so many sectoral and departmental interests, a government-wide policy framework is essential if progress is to be made. A *clear* policy is better than none: a *good* policy best of all.

Increase institutional capacity. The UK has acknowledged strengths here, and DFID does considerable work in this particular area. Others with relevant expertise and contacts include the Prince of Wales Business Leaders Forum, World Bank and other multilateral agencies.

Co-ordinate policy. All governments need to work hard to co-ordinate policy. Issues like tourism usually involve more than one department or ministry (or may touch on various different levels within one department). This adds to the need to work closely together. DFID will work with other UK departments on tourism – and also help key stakeholders strengthen their policy co-ordination at all levels.

Open lines of communication. Governments are well placed to help forge links and foster partnerships across governmental organisations, NGOs and industry representatives.

Offer regular official contacts. A Government-initiated forum for all parties interested in developing nature tourism would deepen understanding and increase all parties' confidence.

Brief media on tourism issues. This is one way for governments to help place tourism on the agenda – and keep it there. Newspaper and TV editors are especially important to reach.

Help identify and disseminate best practice. Particularly to key stakeholders in the south. Governments could also encourage this tendency in northern stakeholders.

Promote a small businesses culture. As governments recognise how much tourism concerns small businesses, they can concentrate on ways to support an entrepreneurial culture, e.g. by removing regulatory barriers, offering formal recognition and sponsoring business associations.

Link institutions. Governments are well placed to sponsor links between key institutions. The UK has significant expertise in managing visitors, and links with national parks in partner countries would be beneficial. Enduring institutional links (so-called 'twinning') are better than short-term exchanges.

Work with umbrella groups. The Association of British Travel Agents (ABTA), Association of International Tour Operators (AITO) and the International Federation of Tour Operators (IFTO) are all useful partners. And an NGO round table may emerge.

Use nature tourism to spread awareness of developing countries. Direct contact creates an audience that is eager to know more.

NGOs

Build bridges. The great strength of NGOs lies in their ability to forge partnerships between stakeholders, to interface with local communities, and to 'put it all together' by providing an overview. Many of the actions below are about building the capacity of NGOs to play up these strengths.

Get up to speed. Use networks, seminars, round tables, etc. to prime other NGOs about the importance of nature tourism to the development and environmental agenda.

Build a reserve of 'intellectual capital' that is robust, workable and applicable.

Lobby for informed change. Continue to act as a conscience, but to get the ball rolling – concentrate on achievable actions. VSO's World Wise campaign shows what can be done.

Foster co-ordination at official levels, i.e. through NGOs' cross-departmental projects and programmes.

Brief media. Regular briefings on tourism issues and NGO action to help raise awareness – at the moment, journalists complain that NGOs don't really understand the news agenda.

Reach consumers with independent messages. Tell them where tourism is going generally – and the specifics of visiting developing countries. Remember that most people want positives, too.

Link industry with UK business advice expertise. NGOs are well placed to broker effective partnerships (e.g. with Enterprise Agencies) to help translate small business expertise across to local community entrepreneurs.

Avoid being too downbeat. People's holidays are hard earned: be careful not to alienate allies.

Develop educational material. Cover behaviour, culture, actions, impacts, choices and so on.

Disseminate information well, i.e. imaginatively and effectively. People rarely read leaflets, but always read guidebooks, tags on sunglasses, health information...

Provide industry with authoritative guidance, e.g. on best practice. This needs to be gathered, agreed, made useful for the target audience – and then disseminated.

Create a (standing) forum on tourism. Several areas need clarifying – especially tensions between NGOs acting as facilitator and operator. Currently, the former is a strength, the latter a weakness.

Create imaginative pilot partnerships, as a blueprint for others.

Consider a joint industry/NGO certification scheme. And push it beyond purely environmental issues.

Develop tourism indicators. Make them realistic, credible and easy to communicate.

Signposts

groups with a tourism focus

centre for environmentally responsible tourism (cert)
T +44 (0)181 761 1910
E certdesk@aol.com

earthwatch europe T +44 (0)1865 311 600
E info@uk.earthwatch.apc.org

the ecotourism society T +1 802 447 2121

survival T +44 (0)171 242 1441
E survival@gn.apc.org

tourism concern T +44 (0)171 753 3330
E tourconcern@gn.apc.org

voluntary services overseas (vso)
T +44 (0)181 780 2266 E jelliott@vso.org.uk

world tourism organisation (wto)
T +34 1571 0628 E omt@dial.eunet.es

world travel and tourism council (wttc)
T +44 (0)171 833 9400
E CreatingJobs@compuserve.com

websites: all @ http://

www.adventuretravel.com
Home to the Adventure Travel Society and Adventure
Travel Trade Association (ATTA) members. Hotlinks to
various publications and other resources.

campfire-zimbabwe.org
Attractive, detailed and informative site about the
Communal Areas Management Programme for
Indigenous Resources (CAMPFIRE), with background,
factsheets as well as links.

www.ecotourism.org
Home of The Ecotourism Society with a wealth of
resources for conservationists, industry and
researchers, includes a virtual 'ecotourism explorer path'!

www.gn.apc.org
GreenNet is quick and easy "for those who don't know
much about computers", has a UK and European focus,
and hosts many relevant organisations.

www.grameen.com
Full details of the Grameen Bank success story, with
background, historical data series, contact details and
links.

www.ids.ac.uk
Institute of Development Studies' Devline – government
research, information resources, databases, the British
Library and more.

www.iied.org
International Institute for Environment and Development – cross-cutting research, insights and ideas.

www.envirolink.org
Index of over 200 subjects – plus hotlinks, bookstore, quick search, magazine lists.

www.mailbase.ac.uk
Electronic discussion lists for the UK Higher Education community.

www.oneworld.org
News, media, action, partners (some 120 international NGOs) – even an e-bazaar. Always accessible, current – and useful.

www.oneworld.org/pwblf/
The Prince of Wales Business Leaders Forum site includes a searchable database with a wealth of information about socially and environmentally responsible businesses and partnerships.

www.podi.com/ecosource
"ecotourism: what's hot – what's not, destinations, tours and operators, lodges and resorts, activities, publications, how to's and how not to's, definitions and more..."

www.sej.org
The Society of Environmental Journalists offers a good selection of links and resources – particularly on the travel media.

www.tourism-montreal.org
Interesting coverage on government tourism, tourism journals and news, associations, resource management, schools and sustainable development.

www.webdirectory.com
"Earth's biggest environment search engine" with an extensive index including government, national parks and sustainable development.

www.worldbank.org
The World Bank has a huge database. "Culture in sustainable development" has documents, concepts, projects, guidelines and resources – and offers a concise précis of the subject.

www.wttc.org
World Travel and Tourism Council (WTTC) hosted ECoNETT rural tourism discussion forum, plus WTTC meeting (September, 1998) papers, resources and hotlinks including international agreements.

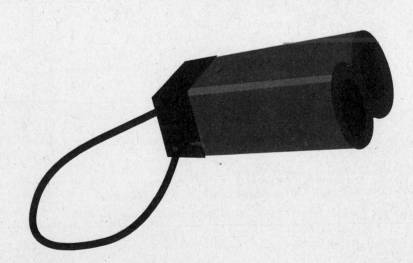

Further reading

magazines to read

Condé Nast Traveller MONTHLY
AVAILABLE FROM NEWSAGENTS
Targeted at a more 'elite' clientele. March 1998 edition
features Ethical Tourism.

The Courier BI-MONTHLY, SUBSCRIPTION ONLY. ACP-EU,
200 RUE DE LA LOI, 1049, BRUSSELS, BELGIUM
Coverage related to the developing world, regular in-
depth features on tourism in a global and regional
context.

Developments DFID. FREE QUARTERLY, SUBSCRIPTION
ONLY. PO BOX 99, WETHERBY, LS23 7JA
Relevant articles in the 1st and 3rd issues of 1998.
Accessible style.

Earthmatters FRIENDS OF THE EARTH. ISSUE 38 – GREEN
TOURISM. TEL: +44 (0)171 490 1555
Developed and developing country destination case
studies plus Charter 88 and sustainable tourism articles.

Geographical THE ROYAL GEOGRAPHICAL SOCIETY
AVAILABLE FROM NEWSAGENTS
Regular conservation and tourism features, plus country
reviews. Extensive ads, news and reviews.

Global Adventure BI-MONTHLY
AVAILABLE FROM NEWSAGENTS
Adventure tourism focus. "Lovely Planet" page on
conservation, tourism and cultural issues, events listing.

In Focus TOURISM CONCERN. TEL: +44 (0)171 753 3330
A valuable information source and networking tool. "In a
class of its own" according to The New Statesman.

Travel Africa Magazine BI-MONTHLY, SUBSCRIPTION ONLY
FREEPOST SCE 6004, OXFORD, OX44 9BR
Useful coverage on tourism ethics, national parks,
conservation, local communities, news and comments.

Wanderlust BI-MONTHLY. AVAILABLE FROM NEWSAGENTS
OR WANDERLUST. TEL: +44 (0)1753 620426
Each edition covers a country or region in detail, plus
short articles on all aspects of the industry.

Worldwise STILL AVAILABLE
VSO. TEL: + 44 (0)181 780 7580
Joint VSO and Guardian travel supplement, accompanied
VSO Fair Trade in Tourism campaign launch.

books to pack

Agenda 21 for the Travel and Tourism Industry: Towards
Environmentally Sustainable Development
WTTC (SEE GROUPS)
Readable post-Rio keynote from WTTC, WTO and the
Earth Council. Includes Agenda 21 summary plus action
framework.

An Analysis of Ecotourism's Economic Contribution to
Conservation and Development in Belize
K. LINDBERG AND J. ENRIQUEZ (1994) WORLD WILDLIFE
FUND, GODALMING
Provides an excellent case study of the financial and
economic impacts of ecotourism.

Ecotourism and Conservation: a review of the issues
K. BRANDON, WORKING PAPER NO 33, WORLD BANK
ENVIRONMENT DEPARTMENT, WASHINGTON DC
Excellent and honest overview of the realities of
ecotourism in terms of opportunities, challenges – and
dogmas.

Tourism, Ecotourism and Protected Areas
H. CEBALLOS-LASCURAIN (1996) IUCN PROTECTED AREAS
PROGRAMME, GLAND
Practical handbook for the industry emerging from 4th
World Congress on National Parks and Protected Areas
(1992).

The Green Travel Guide
G. NEALE (1998) EARTHSCAN, LONDON
Accessible alternative guide by Daily Telegraph
correspondent. Sections on the industry, regions and a
travellers directory.

Ecotourism: A Guide for Planners & Managers
K. LINDBERG AND D. HAWKINS (EDS) (1993) ECOTOURISM
SOCIETY, NORTH BENNINGTON
Highly specific content relevant to professionals, policy-
makers and researchers.

Ecotourism: A Guide for Planners & Managers, Volume 2
K. LINDBERG, M. EPLER WOOD AND D. EAGLEDRUM (EDS)
(1998) ECOTOURISM SOCIETY, NORTH BENNINGTON
Another helping of the same.

Environmental Codes of Conduct for Tourism
UNEP IE (1995) TECHNICAL REPORT NO. 29, PARIS
Detailed directory with a global perspective on travel
industry and host community "codes of conduct". Covers
implementation, monitoring and recommendations.
Includes useful addresses.

The Earthscan Reader in Sustainable Tourism
L. FRANCE (ED) (1997) EARTHSCAN, LONDON
Compilation of expert papers providing a handbook for all
those involved in developing policy recommendations.

Ecotourism in the Less Developed World
D. WEAVER (1998) CAB INTERNATIONAL, WALLINGFORD.
Research resource with case studies from Costa Rica,
Kenya, Nepal, Thailand, the Caribbean and the South
Pacific.

People and Tourism in Fragile Environments
M. PRICE (ED) (1996) WILEY, CHICHESTER
A readable and multidisciplinary collection of case
studies from around the world.

Tourism and Sustainability: New Tourism in the Third World
M. MOWFORTH AND L. MUNT (1998) ROUTLEDGE, LONDON
Asks whether "new forms of tourism offer a means for
Third World countries to escape the confines of
'underdevelopment'?"

Ecotourism: A Sustainable Option?
E. CATER AND G. LOWMAN (EDS) (1994) WILEY,
CHICHESTER
The major issues through a series of case studies.
Contains a very accessible piece on the Annapurna
Conservation Area.

Planning for Sustainable Tourism: The Ecomost Project
INTERNATIONAL FEDERATION OF TOUR OPERATORS (1994)
IFTO, LEWES
Uses research in Mallorca and Rhodes to set out a
sustainable tourism agenda and a series of generic
principles of applicable to all countries. As well as
environmental issues, the economic and social problems
of seasonal tourism are addressed.

Take only Photographs, Leave only Footprints: the
environmental impacts of wildlife tourism
D. ROE, N. LEADER-WILLIAMS AND B. DALAL-CLAYTON
(1997) IIED, LONDON (0171 388 2117).
Review of the research, with particular reference to
environmental impacts at different scales of activity.

Beyond the Green Horizon – principles for sustainable
tourism
S. EBER (ED) (1992) TOURISM CONCERN/WWF,
LONDON/GODALMING
A set of principles and worked examples, with a
particular emphasis on policy issues.

Whose Eden? An overview of community approaches to
wildlife management
IIED (1994) LONDON (0171 388 2117)
Analysis based on real-world examples including
CAMPFIRE. Famously starts with a Larson cartoon.

The Paradise Project: Children's Research on Tourism
in Grenada
Copies from Save the Children Fund UK,
17 Grove Lane, London SE5 8RD. www.scfuk.org.uk

articles to peruse

Managing ecotourism: an opportunity spectrum approach
S. BOYD AND R. BUTLER (1996) TOURISM MANAGEMENT 17:8
Develops and assesses an ecotourism-specific procedure
to look at impacts, management and planning.

Environmental contradictions in sustainable tourism
E. CATER (1995) GEOGRAPHIC JOURNAL 161
Recommends resolving conflict by developing positive
environment, socio-economic and tourism links.

In pursuit of ecotourism
H. GOODWIN (1996) BIODIVERSITY AND CONSERVATION 5
Looks at the emergence of the nature tourism business,
strategies for integrated development and sustainable
economic opportunities for local people.

Managing legitimacy in ecotourism
T. LAWRENCE AND D. WICKENS (1997) TOURISM
MANAGEMENT 18 (5)
The Canadian ecotourism industry is used as an example
to provide a theoretical framework for "legitimacy
management".

Tourism. Key sheet no 2 for development in the natural
environment
ODI/DFID (1997)
Two-page briefing note to get quickly up-to-speed.
Includes issues, seminal literature, contacts and
research.

Tourism, conservation and sustainable development
H. GOODWIN, I. KENT, K. PARKER AND M. WALPOLE (1998)
IIED WILDLIFE AND DEVELOPMENT 12
A detailed account of the DFID research at the heart of
this document.

DFID

The Department for International Development (DFID) is the government department responsible for managing Britain's programme of development assistance to poorer countries and for ensuring that Government policies which affect developing countries, including the environment, trade, investment and agricultural policies, take account of developing country issues.

As set out in its White Paper on International Development, published in November 1997, the Government is committed to the internationally agreed targets to halve the proportion of people living in abject poverty by 2015, together with the associated targets including universal access to primary education and basic health care by the same date.

In July 1998 the Government announced a major increase in its development assistance budget. This will rise from £2,326 million in 1998/99 to £3,218 million in 2001/2. As a percentage of GNP, this should lead to a rise from 0.25% in 1998 to 0.30% in 2001.

DFID will work in partnership with developing countries which are committed to the international targets, and is putting in place new ways of working with the business and voluntary sectors, and the research community.
As well as its Headquarters in London and East Kilbride, DFID has offices in New Delhi, Bangkok, Nairobi, Harare, Pretoria, Dhaka, Suva and Bridgetown.

DFID would like to thank the BBC's Alex Kirby, the International Federation of Tour Operators' Martin Brackenbury, and David Shreeve from The Conservation Foundation for chairing the consultative conferences that helped develop this document.

Typeset in **Franklin Gothic**
Printed on recycled paper: **Sylvancoat**
Put together by **River Path Associates**
(www.riverpath.com) and **Harold Goodwin**
Signposts research by **Julia Leslie**
Graphic illustrations by **Nila Aye**
Design by **3 Men And A Suit**
Printed by **Cedar Colour**

DFID is grateful to the following for their input:
Lloyd Anderson, The British Council • Caroline Ashley, Overseas Development Institute (ODI) • Robert Baldi, Department of the Environment, Transport and the Regions (DETR) • Michael Ball, Symbiosis Expedition Planning • Russel Barlow-Jones, South African Tourism Board • Robert Barrington, Earthwatch • Sylvia Beales, Save the Children Fund • Simon Beeching, Wexas International • Peter Bennet, Rainforest Concern • Oliver Bennett, Deloitte & Touche International • Helen Brown, Rain Forest Concern • Sue Bryant • Kevan Bundell, Christian Aid • Peter Burns, University of Luton • Vanessa Buxton, Alternative Travel Group • Erlet Cater, University of Reading • Bridget Christopher, North-South Travel • Chris Coe, Imagos • Martin Davies, Royal Society for the Protection of Birds (RSPB) • Roger Diski, Rainbow Tours • Louise Dixey, UK Centre for Economic & Environmental Development • Liz Dodd, Action for Southern Africa • Lesley Downer • Toby Durden, Okavango Tours and Safaris • Marian Edmunds, Financial Times • Sobers Esprit, Commonwealth of Dominica • Christine Fagg • Jayne Forbes, Tourism Concern • Shirley Galligan, Born Free Foundation • Louis Godinho, Save Goa Campaign • David Goslett • Susan Grant, The Communications Group • Giles Gurney, European Community Network for Environmental Travel and Tourism (ECoNETT) • Doug Gustafson, International Finance Corporation (IFC) • Miranda Haines, Traveller • Rebecca Hawkins, International Hotels Environment Initiative • Jeff Haynes, Dartmoor National Park Authority • Rob Hitchins, The Springfield Centre for Business in Development • Andrew Holden, University of London Centre for Tourism & Leisure Studies • Angela Humphery • Liz Humphreys, Frontier • Jon Hutton, Africa Resources Trust • David James, Global Tourism Solutions • Wyndham James, Oxfam • Sharon James, Voluntary Services Overseas (VSO) • Mike Kennedy, English Tourist Board • Aline Keuroghlian, Alternative Travel Group • George Kirya, Ugandan High Commission • Julia Leslie • Keith Madders, Zimbabwe Trust • Amanda Marks, Tribes • Lara Marsh, United Nations Environment & Development UK Committee (UNED UK) • Julian Matthews, Discovery Initiatives • Sarah Miller, Condé Nast Traveller • Simon Mlay, Tanzania Trade Centre • Stephen Nattrass • Greg Neale, The Sunday Telegraph • Beatrice Newbery, Orbit • Andrew Ngone, Commonwealth Secretariat • Christine Osborne • Mary Painter, RSPB • Jens Parkitny, Media for Nature • Angela Powell, Centre for Environmentally Responsible Tourism (CERT) • Nick Poynton, Wimberly Allison Tong & Goo (WAT&G) • Peter Raines, Coral Cay Conservation • Ian Reynolds, Association of British Travel Agents (ABTA) • Jake Reynolds, World Conservation Monitoring Centre (WCMC) • Keith Richards, ABTA • Dilys Roe, International Institute for Environment and Development (IIED) • John Ruler • Margot Sallows, Green Globe International • Patrick Simkin • Lisa Sykes, The Sunday Times • Richard Tapper, Environment, Business & Development Group • Juan Tirado, Embassy of Peru • Mark Toogood, Centre for the Study of Environmental Change (CSEC) • Jonathon Vernon-Powell, Nomadic Thoughts Worldwide Travel • John Ward, Travel & Tourism Programme • Michael Woods.

Please accept our apologies if we have left you off this list.